I0493025

GOT MEDIA?

A Mini Preparation Handbook

for

Powerfully Positioning Your

Media Success

Alicia "WATERS"

Got Media?

Copyright © 2016 Alicia Nicole "WATERS"

www.amazon.com/author/alicianwaters
anwempires@gmail.com
ISBN:13: 978-1533269751

Printed in the United States of America by Kindle Direct Publishing

Got Media?

Dedication & Acknowledgments

This is a general dedication to those who desire to get started with using the media to bring more exposure to their brand. This is also for those who are already in the media but would like to up-level their efforts.

This publication is designed to encourage those who are in influential roles to utilize the power of the media to their highest advantage to bring more exposure to their brand and/or business.

I give thanks and acknowledgments to God and to every person, product or process that has helped me to take my media agenda to the next level.

Got Media?

Table of Contents

Introduction
Got Media?

Media is one of the biggest and probably the most influential mediums of all time. It has evolved throughout the years and has been a very valuable and effective vehicle of expression for many. Though it has pros and cons, when used in the most positive manner, great change can occur to impact the lives of many.

Whether you are a speaker, trainer, author or entrepreneur, using media in various forms is vital to making a huge impact through outreach. The effects of multimedia have been proven throughout each era of change to be the most effective gateway for reaching the masses in a huge way. The media also creates greater expansion to one's mission and/or movement.

I've always been very fascinated with the media arts since I was a little girl. I can remember starting my own pretend radio station in my room with my boom box.

Got Media?

I would produce shows, DJ the best songs and use my brother and friends as staff. I would also use my gifts of acting to imitate celebrity guests to do interviews.

Because I've always been into performing arts, doing presentations, singing, acting and modeling came so easy to me. Being in the public eye was never really a challenge for me. I was use to getting featured in the newspaper or having small clips of something I would be involved in get featured on the local news. Often, I would be a regular caller on radio shows as a frequent winner of prizes. I realized at a young age that media was a powerful tool for exposure.

I loved the media so much that I went to tech school to obtain a certification in radio and television broadcasting. During my time there, I was able to land a great internship as a newscaster at a radio station and later went on to produce my very own live talk show on that same station once my intern was complete.

Got Media?

After that experience, I furthered my education by going to Bible college where I earned a Bachelor of Science in Bible and a concentration in Media Communications.

Throughout the years these experiences have shown me that if you want to be most effective in what you do, the media must be at the forefront of your agenda. There's just no way of getting around it. Media has and will always be the greatest agent of change for truly reaching the masses at the highest level.

Now of course you don't have to be a media or communications graduate to be effective or even be an authority in the multimedia industry. In fact, I truly believe that those who have less formal training and develop their true authentic presence through life and/or hands on experience often are the ones to be most effective with what they do.

There were several years that I spent time away from being in the media in the traditional way. I believe this actually benefited me more in order to do what I'm doing now as a journalism/media communications mentor and business owner of an empire that features

Got Media?

several multimedia platforms. I am also the founder of several multimedia ministry platforms.

As mentioned previously, the traditional formats, though helpful for training, actually became sort of a small hindrance to what was emerging next for me as an entrepreneur. When I learned how to step away from the traditional path and began using media from an entrepreneurial vantage point, everything changed. I also saw how I could help others with no media background become a media and/or multimedia marketing authority within their niche to create change and greater expansion for their vision and/or outreach.

This publication will provide a simplistic, yet up-leveled approach for how to amp up the basics of getting started with media and/or taking your media exposure agenda to the next levels of success.

Again, I'm extremely passionate about sharing on the importance and effectiveness of media. I feel that every person whether in a traditional or nonlinear leadership role (any great influential person), should really use the power of media to advance their mission.

Got Media?

I produced this mini handbook to help build true confidence and competence by simplifying the process for the beginner as well as the seasoned. I will also invite you throughout the reading to consider joining me on a continual up-leveling experience for your overall media success as your media mentor in some form.

As you read through this handbook, I'm going to encourage you connect with your inner childlike essence so that you can begin to express yourself, create and/show up in your truest unique form at this phase. There's something about trusting your process of life in a childlike way that brings a sense of greater adventure and/or allows you to dream and create from a realm of infinite possibilities.

So just imagine that you are creating and/or experiencing having a dynamic media presence like never before and making an impact globally through sharing your gifts. It's time to get the results you desire through media. So, get started or restarted today and be prepared.

Got Media?

Great opportunities can come at any time and people will ask you for your media press kit, samples of you being featured in the media and/or inquiring for you to be interviewed.

So, the next time someone asks you if you've got media, you can confidently say yes and provide them with your media press offerings because you're prepared.

SO, ASK YOURSELF, GOT MEDIA?

Got Media?

Got Media? Get Momentum

One of the biggest hold ups that most will experience besides fear when it comes to being featured in the media is simply getting started or restarted after they've been away from the process for a while. I can recall my own experience of spending several years where I wasn't using my gifts in media like I had previously or either not in the way that I had planned.

I felt like I had lost ground for a while and needed to somehow get restarted again and regain the momentum required in order for me to catapult my efforts. One the best ways that I found to be most helpful for getting back into the media was to start my own online radio show. I also found it helpful to start getting featured on a few other online radio platforms hosted by friends and colleagues who had a show.

Stepping up and stepping out to get more exposure to your brand or as an expert can take a lot of courage and certainly requires your mindset, skill set and actions to be congruent to achieve your overall success.

Got Media?

Getting out in the media as mentioned previously in the introduction is very critical and actually non-negotiable as it relates to building and/or up-leveling your brand as well as showcasing your offerings, services and expertise.

The best thing to do is to just get started or restarted and build up the momentum in your media agenda. Once you get the process in motion you will begin to build upon and up-level your media plan. Developing powerful momentum doesn't have to be hard in fact it can be a very easy process.

Once you align, organize and coordinate your media goals, you can begin to jump-start the success that you want and keep the right momentum going at every phase.

Got Media?

3 Ways to Get Media Momentum with Ease

• **Enroll accountability:** Get a mentor, coach or enroll in a media group to help you set goals, and provide you with extra guidance, training and support.

• **Create a simple media press page on your website:** Even if you don't have any interviews, blogs or magazine articles to post, make it a coming soon or upcoming events page. Include a short bio with a few things about yourself, your picture (head-shot preferred) and some of the topics that you will cover in the future or list any of your current or upcoming events.

If you already have a press page and have been doing this for a while but want to get back into it, create yourself a get it done day to revamp what you have, work on your signature talk, write a series articles to have on hand to submit to magazines. Write on your blog and reach out to other blogs to become a guest blogger.

Got Media?

- **Get featured in the media:** Guest blogging, hosting tele-seminars and/or start getting on podcasts is a great way to get started. Whether by doing your own show or being a guest on a few platforms will help you to create momentum.

   Visit websites like www.Blogtalkradio.com and find shows that will be a great fit for your delivery style and expertise. Next, reach out to the hosts of the shows via their website and request to be a guest on their platform.

   Also, ask friends and colleagues to interview you. Even if they don't have a talk show, have them to interview you on a conference line. Next, try to get recommendations or testimonial from them about why you make a great guest for shows. After, upload the recording unto your media press page and include the testimonials.

Got Media?

Are You Seriously Ready to

Get Media Momentum?

Consider:
Multimedia Readiness Made Easy

This platform provides mentoring, publications, and resources for accurate preparation and readiness for your multimedia endeavors.

Visit:
www.multimediareadinessmadeeasy.blogspot.com

Got Media?

Powerfully Positioned
for Media Success

Having the right media and marketing alignment is very critical to one's overall success in the media arena. The most common mistake made by speakers, authors and entrepreneurs is putting themselves out in the media without understanding fully what it takes in order to achieve and sustain success as well as knowing what venues to explore.

Once you step into the spotlight, you want to make sure that you have a powerful presence that exudes the epitome of ownership in your area of expertise. You also want to make sure that you are being seen as the authority in your arena and as one who sets your industry standard. It's important to get the right recognition through being properly positioned you for greater opportunities.

There are seven key areas that I call the pillars to help powerfully position you in the media and will help you catapult your media success.

Got Media?

These areas are preparation, presentation, public speaking, podcasting, publishing, publicity and profits. I will provide the core focuses of these seven areas later in this chapter so that you can explore your options and make your plan of action in the journal planning section located in the back of the book.

Even though all of these areas are important, I recommend working on only your major two or three areas at a time. If you're just beginning, only choose to master one major area with maybe a minor area. I feel this would be the best way to begin the process.

Example: Choose to focus on podcasting as a major to get your feet wet with being interviewed or hosting a show. Your minor could be in publishing for working on your first book project as you are learning the ends and outs of the media.

If you're a seasoned professional I would recommend up-leveling two major areas and one minor or vice versa. Example: You could select the major areas of public speaking to work on your current or new talk while also working on your profits and minor

Got Media?

in the area of publicity by delegating that area to an agent, publicists or marketing manager.

Make sure that you choose the most aligned areas to work on first. Once you get in the flow and begin to create some results, incorporate your next phase. Soon you will be using all seven pillars to amp up your success consistently. Being consistent is very critical for achieving and sustaining results.

Before you get started with your planning, take a look at the *7 Pillars for Powerfully Positioning in the Media* to better understand the core focus of each area in their simplest form. Next, you will be ready to begin taking your media agenda to the next level. Create an aligned plan of action to implement and enroll the right mentor to assist you with the process.

Use the journal planning section in the back to design your next levels of media success and beyond.

Got Media?

7 Powerful Pillars for Positioning in the Media

Preparation

Presentation

Public Speaking

Podcasting

Publishing

Publicity

Profits

Each of these seven areas must be mastered effectively at every phase of your journey in order to continuously elevate your success. An overview and objectives are provided for you to gain clarity on the core focus of each area.

Once you understand the primary chief aim of these seven pillars you can begin to craft your success. In addition, do your research, align with the right mentor and/or programs/products.

Got Media?

Preparation
Mastering Your Media Mindset & Master Planning

Presentation
The Art of Mastering Presence & Performance

Public Speaking
Effective Communications to Live Audiences

Podcasting
Online Expert Teaching/Speaking & Interviews

Publishing
Mastering Written Communications as an Expert

Publicity
Media Exposure via Online/Offline Platforms

Profits
Making Revenue through Your Media Efforts

Got Media?

Preparation

Preparation is the ongoing process of being mentality, skillfully and confidently ready for your success. Though being a master craftsman at your expertise is critical to your success, mindset mastery for media is even more vital. You must continuously cultivate your mind for being ready for the media.

Your preparation process should include not only your master planning process, but also a mindset and competence challenge for every phase. In turn, this will begin to increase your confidence. You can also implement more effectively by breaking down your tasks into small goals with deadlines.

Accurately Prepare: You must be clear about your media goals and your target audience: Clarity, commitment and consistency are the keys to your short, mid and long term success. Write down your primary chief aim or intention for the results and impact that you desire to make. Working correctly in alignment with your goals is very important. Again, you want to make sure that you prepare accurately.

Got Media?

Presentation

Presentation is more than just what you are presenting in terms of content or delivery style, it's about mastering your presence on all levels. Mastering your total essence for how you will show up in the media is the main key component to not only landing great and worthwhile opportunities but keeping and increasing them as well.

Your presence should exude the epitome of not only your expertise but also your overall way of BEING that will come through your personality and/or your communications. This should be demonstrated in your copy, content, social media presence including what's on your website and most of all powerfully through your presentation. Mastering your presence starts with knowing your true authentic self. Once you know your true authentic self, begin to serve, share and sell from that higher vantage point.

Once you've become a master of your overall presence, your presentations will begin to make a stronger connection to your target audience and win over loyal followers who will know, like and trust you.

Got Media?

Public Speaking

Public speaking for most, is probably one of the most fearful arenas to embark on. Even for several who have been doing public speaking for years still get nervous. They continue to overcome newer levels for gaining more confidence at every new phase of their success. Over the last several years, public speaking has been one of the most effective communications styles that truly connects speakers with their target audience.

Traditionally public speaking is done in the form of live seminars or conferences held at different venues to groups that vary in size. Recently, the newer emergence for public speaking in an unconventional way is to use your everyday life. Whether you're at the store, networking event or at any social gathering you can be used as an opportunity to do public speaking.

It's still a form of making a live connection to add value through a conversational style mini talk. This will help you to always be confidently prepared for all public speaking opportunities and increase your credibility towards your brand, and/or business.

Got Media?

Podcasting

Podcasting is one of the most effective media mediums for speakers, leaders, authors, entrepreneurs and small business owners to make a huge global impact with their works. Over the years, the internet has made the world a lot smaller by creating virtual experiences that allow those who are in influential roles to globally spread their messages all over.

Podcasting provides communicators with many opportunities to share their expertise as a top online authority in their industry. Using online radio in this manner powerfully positions experts to showcase their brand, business and/or networks to multiple audience worldwide. It's a great way for beginners and veteran podcasters to either build and/or up-level the areas of communications, brand establishment and notoriety.

Explore different podcast outlets to either launch a new show, up-level your current podcast, or request to be a guest for an interview. This is one of the fastest and most effective ways to gain the media exposure that you desire.

Got Media?

Publishing

Publishing is an effective way to master one's communications through written expression as an expert. Being published is one of the most vital areas to have under your belt for powerfully positioning your media success. There is just something about a person being published that makes different industries and the public take notice of one's works, brand, or business. Publishing levels up your communications in written format.

It's also one of the fastest and most credible ways to get recognition in the media. Whether it's through publishing books, blogging, writing articles for other magazines or starting your own, people want to hear your stories and how you can best help them to reach their greater success.

If you're not published, get published right away even if it's publishing a mini version of your bigger book. Blog/guest blog, start an e-zine or even your own magazine. This will open up doors in a huge way for your media success as a recognized publisher.

Got Media?

Publicity

Publicity is the main key ingredient to your media success. It doesn't matter how prepared you are or how great your products or services are if the right people don't know about it. Getting out in the media and having your brand recognized, received and also remembered is what will make you standout as remarkable.

It's not enough just to have a lot of publicity. You must have aligned publicity and be presenting your message to the right audience. As mentioned in the preparation process, you must have accurately prepared for effectively showcasing yourself to the right audience. This is true with publicity. Getting the right media exposure is what will catapult your media success.

You can rightly align your publicity efforts by enrolling the right team, exploring media outlets that will best serve your niche and/or gain access to a media directory with outlets to submit your press.

Got Media?

Profits

Profiting through your media efforts is more important than most would think. It's more than just having resources to create a better lifestyle and/or pay off debts. You can't effectively advance your success or take your brand or business to the next levels if you aren't making meaningful (more than enough) profits through your current media exposure efforts that will allow you to expand your brand.

One of the best ways to powerfully position yourself for profits is to get present and start to focus on designing a higher-level profits model for your short, mid and long-term media success. Profiting through media, often requires planning with sort of a reverse-engineering process of thinking with the end in mind.

This involves up-leveling your clarity of vision along with having a clear concise plan for achieving your higher impact and income goals. However, being detached from the unfolding to allow better profitable opportunities to manifest through your media efforts.

Got Media?

Afterword
Got Media? Get Results

After reading this handbook you've come to realize the greater importance of truly being accurately prepared for getting the right media exposure. If you've gained nothing else from any of the other concepts or the seven pillars in this book, allow the process of accurate preparation to become the one core element of your driving force for excellence.

The late and great defense attorney, Johnny Cochran use to repeat often; "Preparation, preparation, preparation is the key to your success." I agree, that it's better to be over prepared and over deliver rather than be under prepared and fall short.

Though preparation is critical, you must begin the process of implementing and executing in order to get results. It's not enough just to have the right media alignment, you must consistently be willing to show up and participate in your next levels of success to get the results. So now that you've got your media plan, go get results.

Got Media?

BONUS PODCAST FEATURE

Powerfully Positioning Yourself to Profit with Media with Alicia Nicole "WATERS" on Accelerate Your Business Growth Radio 2016.

Alicia Nicole "WATERS" shared on Accelerate Your Business Growth radio about how to accurately prepare to position yourself to profit with the media by designing a higher-level profits model.

Type the YouTube link below into your browser to listen and enjoy!

https://www.youtube.com/watch?v=Bw_vI37cKJ4

Got Media?

Got Media Momentum?
Success Planning Section

Media Momentum

Plan of Action

Got Media?

More Notes:

Got Media?

Media Momentum

Plan of Action

Got Media?

More Notes:

Got Media?

Media Momentum

Plan of Action

Got Media?

More Notes:

Got Media?

Media Momentum

Plan of Action

Got Media?

More Notes:

Got Media?

Media Momentum

Plan of Action

Got Media?

More Notes:

Got Media?

Media Momentum

Plan of Action

Got Media?

More Notes:

Got Media?

Media Momentum

Plan of Action

Got Media?

More Notes:

Got Media?

Media Momentum

Plan of Action

Got Media?

More Notes:

Got Media?

Media Momentum

Plan of Action

Got Media?

More Notes:

Got Media?

Media Momentum

Plan of Action

Got Media?

More Notes:

Got Media?

Media Momentum

Plan of Action

Got Media?

More Notes:

Got Media?

More Notes:

Got Media?

Media Momentum

Plan of Action

Got Media?

More Notes:

Got Media?

Media Momentum

Plan of Action

Got Media?

More Notes:

Got Media?

Media Momentum

Plan of Action

More Notes:

Got Media?

Media Momentum

Plan of Action

Got Media?

More Notes:

Got Media?

Media Momentum

Plan of Action

Got Media?

More Notes:

Got Media?

Media Momentum

Plan of Action

Got Media?

More Notes:

Got Media?

More Notes:

Got Media?

Write a Brief Summary About Your Process

Got Media?

Summary Continued:

Got Media?

About the Author

Alicia Nicole "WATERS", features in the media over 500 online platforms for different industries and is a published author of over 200 journal style trainers. She is also the founder of several multimedia ministry platforms.

She serves in roles such as a cross-industries journalist, multi-niche speaker, media communications mentor, and multimedia personality.

She is a graduate/alumnus of Trenholm State Technical College where she earned a certification in Radio & Television Broadcasting. A graduate/alumnus of Johnson University (formerly Johnson Bible College) where she earned a Bachelor of Science in Bible & Media Communications.

Got Media?

For More Resources

www.multimediareadinessmadeeasy.blogspot.com

www.amazon.com/author/alicianwaters

Or

To Book the Author

For Speaking Engagements

Email: anwempires@gmail.com

If you enjoyed this resource, please consider writing a review on Amazon.com

Thanks & Blessings!

Got Media?